Chimney sweeps with their handcart in Paddington around 1900. The badges on their caps would show the name and address of the master sweep.

Chimneys and
Chimney Sweeps

Benita Cullingford

A Shire book

CONTENTS

Cover: *A nineteenth-century illustration of a chimney sweep. (By courtesy of Ken Bryant, Chimmobilia, Chimney Sweep Collectibles, Castle Cary, Somerset)*

British Library Cataloguing in Publication Data: Cullingford, Benita. Chimneys and Chimney Sweeps. – (Shire album; 415) 1. Chimneys – History 2. Chimney sweeps – History I. Title 697.8'09 ISBN 0 7478 0553 9.

ACKNOWLEDGEMENTS
Illustrations are acknowledged as follows: Ken Bryant, page 4; Cadbury Lamb, pages 5 (bottom right), 9 (bottom), 27 (bottom), 31 (top two); Leeds Museums & Galleries, pages 22 (bottom) and 23; Numatic International Ltd, page 30 (bottom); Ramoneur Company, pages 25 (top) and 28; Lord Salisbury, page 10 (both). Other illustrations are from the author's collection or are photographs by the author.

Published in 2003 by Shire Publications Ltd, Cromwell House, Church Street, Princes Risborough, Buckinghamshire HP27 9AA, UK. (Website: www.shirebooks.co.uk)
Copyright © 2003 by Benita Cullingford. First published 2003. Shire Album 415. ISBN 0 7478 0553 9.
Benita Cullingford is hereby identified as the author of this work in accordance with Section 77 of the Copyright, Designs and Patents Act 1988.
Printed in Great Britain by CIT Printing Services Ltd, Press Buildings, Merlins Bridge, Haverfordwest, Pembrokeshire SA61 1XF.

INTRODUCTION

On 25th June 1817, a bill to prevent the further use of climbing boys in sweeping chimneys was introduced to Parliament. The following evidence is taken from a *Report from the Committee of the House of Commons.*

London master sweep John Cook, from Windmill Street, was called in and examined. He began his apprenticeship when he was six years old and had been thirty-two years in the trade.

Question: Do you employ climbing boys at present? – Yes.

Question: Do you not also employ a machine? – Yes.

Question: What sum of money is generally given for those children to the parents by the master sweep? – £2 or £3, it depends upon circumstances. Sometimes more sometimes less.

Question: Do you give more for children that are delicately formed and who therefore are better calculated for ascending small chimneys? – The smaller they are the master generally likes them the better...

Question: For what chimneys do you use the climbing boys in preference to the new machine? – There are so many people against the machine who will not let them come into the house. I should lose their custom. I am obliged to keep boys as well as the machine.

A master sweep buying an apprentice. As shown in the frontispiece to James Montgomery's 'Climbing-Boy's Album' (1824), impoverished mothers were still selling small children to master sweeps. The first Chimney Sweeping Act was passed in 1788. The act banned the apprenticing of children under the age of eight years, but the law could not be enforced.

Question: Is the trade unhealthy? – No; I think it is healthy ... I have had them (boys) very sickly when they come to me ... I had a lad apprenticed to me out of St James's parish, and when he came to me he had a bad head, and bad knees, and bad breath; now that boy was not at work more than six or seven months before three or four worms came away, which the soot drove from him and cleared his inside.

The committee heard evidence from a further fourteen witnesses, and the bill was passed. It failed, nevertheless, when it reached the House of Lords. Despite the invention of machines, boys continued to climb chimneys until 1875 when the fifth and final Chimney Sweeping Act was passed. To appreciate why boys were needed for so long it is helpful to understand the reason for chimneys being built, and to know something about the construction and development of chimney flues.

The comic postcard view of the Victorian chimney sweep did not reflect the harsh working conditions.

THE DEVELOPMENT OF CHIMNEYS

In medieval Britain, when life was becoming more sophisticated, greater comfort was called for. In dwellings where smoke from a central hearth, rising on a current of warmed air, was left to find its own way out of rafters and gaps in walls the discomfort was considerable. The solution was a chimney. Smoke could be channelled inside a chimney flue and guided to a suitable exit.

In castles, a funnel-shaped flue was cut through the thickness of stone walls. The flue sloped backwards and upwards at an angle of 45 degrees. Thirteenth-century castles such as Chirk Castle, Wrexham, Wales, had vertical chimneys built into their battlements. Vertical flues – because of the wind's back-pressure – were more successful because smoke was less likely to drift backwards. Chimneys were one storey in height, either from the ground or first floor, and contained a single vertical flue.

Fireplaces were fitted with stone collecting hoods or canopies. In the Abbot's Kitchen at Glastonbury Abbey, Somerset, there are four corner fireplaces. Their flues are carried up the walls and gathered in the roof area into an octagonal lantern.

Fragments of thirteenth-century chimney-pots have been found. Discoveries at Lewes and Chichester in Sussex show that the pots were made of clay and had decorative markings and holes below the rim, where smoke could escape. A 'chymenea terr' (earthen chimney) was bought for the Palace of Westminster in 1278 from Ralph de Crokerelane (south of Fleet Street) for the sum of 5d. The cost of a pot eighty-five years later in 1363, when purchased for the smoke vent of the King's Hall,

Below left: *The Jew's House, Lincoln, dating from 1170. The original fireplace was positioned in the hall on the first floor.*

Below right: *The late-fourteenth-century Abbot's Kitchen at Glastonbury, Somerset, is one of the best-preserved medieval kitchens in England. It has fireplaces at each of the four corners.*

Fireplaces in the abbot's lounge, Kirkstall Abbey, Leeds, c.1230. From the mid twelfth century two fireplaces stood back to back on one side of the kitchen. A meat kitchen was built in the fifteenth century, when the monks changed from a vegetarian diet to eating meat three times a week. Meat was either roasted or boiled on two hearths.

Rayleigh Park, Essex, was 1s 2d.

Chimney-pots were designed to increase the velocity of ascent of the smoke by reducing the cross-sectional area of the outlet, to minimise the effect of down draught by reducing the area acted on by the wind, and to promote updraught by creating a cross draught inside the upper part of the chimney.

Large chimney-stacks containing many flues completely altered house design. Previously, dwellings were little more than a 'hall', the word being applied to the main living room regardless of size. During the Norman period, the central hearth was moved to the upper end of the hall, where the lord sat with his family. When screens (or partitions) were placed across the width of the hall, the hearth was effectively isolated in a narrow corridor known as a 'smoke bay'. The timber-framed screens were plastered on the inside, with a space in one side for the hearth. The next step was to fashion a smoke 'hood' above the hearth. Hoods or 'canopies' varied but all tapered towards the roof.

(Far left) Packesham, Surrey, 1291–1310. Pots tapered from 15 inches to 10 inches (25–38 cm) at the top. The pot represented was probably used with an open timber roof, associated with a hall built by Sir Eustace de Hacche. (Near left) An early-fourteenth-century pot from Watling Street, London.

6

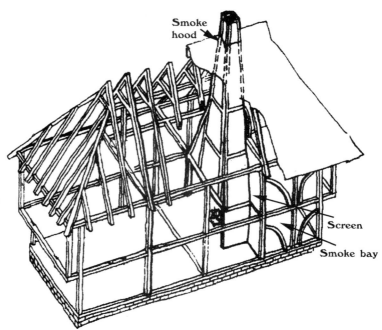

Hall-house conversion: smoke chambers were made by placing two screens or partitions across the width of the hall. Reaching from floor to rafters, they were timber-framed and plastered on the inside. Smoke hoods or canopies, fashioned above the fire, tapered upwards through the roof.

Smoke hood

Screen

Smoke bay

At the lower end of the hall, doors placed either side of the hall created enough draught to keep the fire blazing. Screens were introduced to control the draught and the arrangement was known as the 'cross-passage'. A description of the old fourteenth-century hall in Smithills Manor, Lancashire, reveals that its open timber roof was 'one of great beauty ... and across the westerly end of the hall were screens measuring 35 feet by 25 feet'. Both the smoke bay and the cross-passage afforded good positions for chimney-stacks. When a chimney-stack was inserted in the smoke bay it created a small room behind the hearth, which was fitted with a fireplace.

The gradual process of becoming two-storey was achieved when partial flooring was inserted over the ground-floor screens. Particularly in town houses, the 'solar' or second storey overhung the street to give maximum space to an upstairs room. The hazards of chimney fires and a pressing need for more fireplaces led to the adoption of brick-built stacks.

Brickmaking came into its own in the fifteenth century. Bricks were popular as a building material because they could be made locally and were cheaper to produce than stone. Because bricks were non-combustible, brick-built stacks could be inserted into timber-framed houses. In 1534, the Old Parsonage (now How Dell School, Hatfield, Hertfordshire) already had chimneys. An estimate for repairs, including chimneys, reads: 'The amending of all the chimnies as well as in the backs of them as hearths ... £3.' After 1580, because of fire risk, many timber-framed houses were rebuilt. In 1582 Oxford citizens were reminded of a statute stipulating that roofs should be covered with slate or tile and that all chimneys made of earth or other matter be taken down.

An internal brick chimney-stack could accommodate many flues. Ends of joists, buried in the flue walls, jambs and bressummers made it possible for upper storeys to extend across the entire house, thereby adding an upper room and reducing the loftiness of the hall to 7 or 9 feet (2.1 or 2.7 metres) above the ground. All rooms were

The fifteenth-century chimney on the gatehouse of Rye House, Hoddesdon, Hertfordshire, has a spiral motif and decorative cap. The fireplace below it protrudes from the wall.

fitted with a fireplace. To improve draught, early brick stacks sloped inwards above the fireplace lintel on three sides, course by course, with the back remaining vertical. Where possible, fireplaces – each with an individual flue – were placed back to back inside the stack. The flues narrowed on reaching the roof, terminating together in an extended shaft, their chimney-pots indicating the number of flues.

In *The English Home* (1956), Doreen Yarwood writes: 'In Henry VIII's reign [1509–47] the fireplace was generally let into a wall and the advent of tall chimneys became a typical Tudor innovation.' In country areas, such as Devon, to save space inside, yeoman farmers built chimney-stacks with large supporting buttresses on the outside wall of their cottages.

Chenies Manor, Buckinghamshire, was built with bricks made from clay dug from a nearby field c.1460. Its twenty-two ornamental chimneys date from 1523.

At Coleman Green, Hertfordshire, all that remains of a cottage demolished in 1877 is this chimney-stack. A plaque on the buttress reads 'John Bunyan is said by tradition to have preached and occasionally to have lived in the cottage of which this chimney was a part'. John Bunyan died in 1688. (The John Bunyan Inn nearby shows the cottage chimney on its painted sign.)

In the 1600s, the hall house was made larger by adding a cross-wing set at right angles to the existing house. The wing contained four rooms, two on each level, the upper floors extending beyond the lower. On the opposite side to the entrance, a stairway built against the chimney-stack allowed access to the upper rooms. This type of house became known as the 'axial-stack' house.

By the seventeenth century most houses had chimneys. As Valentine Fletcher says in *Chimney Pots and Stacks*, 'a room without a chimney was considered unfit for guests'. Chimneys became status symbols. Regarded as personal property, they were often mentioned in wills. Although 'chimney' in this context probably meant the fireback and grate, the stack was often left standing when a house was pulled down. At Thundridgebury (Hertfordshire) a chimney-stack was left so that the family could retain their right to a pew in the adjacent church.

At Hampton Court, Cardinal Wolsey's palace, dating from 1525, was rebuilt by Henry VIII and remodelled on similar lines in 1540. Hampton Court was Henry's fourth favourite out of a total of sixty houses. He spent 811 days at the palace during his reign of thirty-eight years. The imposing ornamental chimneys are built of red brick and have diamond patterning picked out in black.

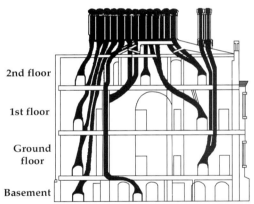

2nd floor

1st floor

Ground
floor

Basement

The west-wing chimneys on the roof of Hatfield House, Hertfordshire, are outlets for the internal flues shown in the diagram. Brick-built in 1608–12, Lord Salisbury's house still possesses eighty-three impressive chimneys. (Reproduced by kind permission of Lord Salisbury.)

Chimneys on country estates could be viewed from miles around. Displaying fine brickwork in ornamental patterns, their tall hexagonal shafts were often twisted or set at angles. Out of sight, flues travelled through the thickness of walls, up perhaps six storeys from basement to attic. On reaching an outlet they terminated in ranks of chimneys, creating an impressive rooftop display.

The kitchen fireplace was common to all homes. In addition to providing heat, large hearths – up to 10 feet (3 metres) across – were used for cooking, roasting, and boiling water. Pots were suspended over the fire by means of a chimney crane, and ovens with iron doors were built into the walls on either side of the fire. Simple tinder-boxes hung beside the hearth. In 1626, Nicholas Breton wrote: 'The servant is stirring betimes, and slipping on her shoes and petticoat, gropes for the tinder box, where after a conflict between the steel and the stone she begets a flame.'

Parlour fireplaces and those in bedchambers were usually five-sided, the deep back wall and splayed sides allowing radiated heat to be pushed forward into the room. They were smaller than that of the kitchen. Used for heating only, they periodically

An example of an ornate stone fireplace surmounted by a carved oak chimney-piece, c.1600.

remained unlit. In baronial halls, chimney-piece mantels of marble or stone were ornately decorated. They displayed family crests, scrolls and gilding. The Italian Renaissance influenced Inigo Jones, and other designers, who made them.

Increased comfort meant a 'hearthpenny fumage' payable on every hearth. Even in Anglo-Saxon times all but the poorest in the community had to pay 'Smoke Farthings', the tax being an important part of the king's revenue. A further hearth tax imposed in 1662 stipulated that householders should pay 2 shillings (20p) for every hearth; payable in two half-yearly instalments. Cottages were exempt. On 18th October 1666 Samuel Pepys recorded in his diary: 'One moved that the chimney money might be taken from the King.' William and Mary repealed the tax in 1689, even though it produced £170,000 in revenue each year.

In a superstitious age, chimneys and fireplaces became receptacles for sacrifices. When Lauderdale House, Highgate, London, was built in the 1600s four chickens, a candlestick and a plaited rush thong were bricked into a chimney recess in the first-floor fireplace. Two of the chickens were buried alive. Their mummified remains were discovered during house renovations in the 1960s. Other customs – thought to be lucky – involved the burial of shoes.

EARLY CHIMNEY-SWEEPING

Smoke from a well-lit fire travels up a hot flue until it reaches an outlet. However, when the fire dies down, the flue cools; cold air rushes in and smoke fumes thicken and congeal, forming soot. Before the extensive use of coal there were many ways of sweeping chimneys. Methods differed because chimneys varied and the assorted fuel that was burned produced different kinds of soot.

Wide chimneys that were short and straight could be cleared of soot by standing in the fireplace with a long-handled broom. The broom, made of birch twigs tied together with a thong, was inserted up the chimney – an easy task for a household servant.

With longer flues, a bundle of rushes on the end of a pliable pole was pushed up from the fireplace, then down from the chimney-top. A country method for tall narrow chimneys was to place a bundle of straw or driftwood inside the chimney then raise and lower it by means of a rope. Depending on the flue's width, a small holly bush or fir-tree was adequate. A similar top-to-bottom technique was carried out with a long pole. The pole was rammed down the chimney to dislodge impacted lumps of tar.

Another approach involved the use of geese and ducks. A bird would be dropped down the flue from the roof, then pulled back up again by a rope attached to its neck. Its powerful wings would loosen the soot as it struggled. (The blacker the bird, the cleaner the chimney.)

Flues had to be scraped. This was because wood – as a result of its water content – produced soot, which clumped together and hardened into a tar-like crust. In districts with stone cottages, chimneys were deliberately set on fire to burn off the soot. Straw was lit in the hearth or the chimney was 'fired' by letting off a shotgun up the flue. Chimneys were often constructed with this incendiary method in mind.

Houses higher than a single storey required the services of a professional sweep. To clean efficiently, the sweep climbed the full length of the chimney flue, sweeping down soot with a hand brush or dislodging impacted soot with a scraper.

Chimney-sweeping was usually carried out by itinerant sweeps roaming the countryside looking for work. 'Chymney Swepers and Costerde Mongers' are first

Silver tokens were used at the time of Charles I in 1632. They were 1 inch (25 mm) in diameter and depicted London trades. The reverse side was decorated with a different floral design. The 'chimney sweepe' was number eighteen out of a set of thirty-six. Between 1649 and 1672, to supplement the lack of small change, traders and innkeepers issued tokens, which showed their name and trade, for use as unofficial money.

Woodcut prints from the seventeenth century show the clothes and equipment of the chimney sweeps' trade. In addition to the bundle of sticks and twigs, the sweep holds a long, pointed stick and scraper.

mentioned in *Cocke Lorell's Bote*, a narrative poem written *c.*1510. Chimney sweeps are also referred to in the dramatic works of Shakespeare, Marlowe and Jonson.

In December 1519, chimney sweep John Scott was paid 2d for 'swepying of ye Kechyn chymnye' in Hunstanton Manor, Norfolk. John Scott lived nearby in Ringstead village. In June 1582, Oxfordshire householders were warned that they would be fined 34d if their chimneys caught fire. Under statutory law they were instructed to sweep their chimneys 'fower [four] tymes everie yeare'. Towards the end of the sixteenth century, the average charge was 2d (1p) for sweeping small chimneys and 7d (3.05p) for large kitchen chimneys.

During the reign of James I (1603–25) there were approximately 150,000 inhabitants in London. The city's premier market-place was Cheapside, where the traders' narrow timber-framed shops were packed together on either side of the thoroughfare. Premises of three to six storeys had tall vertical chimneys. Chimney fires were common.

Many of the city's sweeps lived just north of Cheapside in Old Street and Rotten Row. In 1618, the sweeps sent a petition to the king. They alleged that because of the 'general neglect by householders of their own and the City's safety', there were two hundred of them who 'were ready to be starved for want of work'. They asked that an overseer might be appointed for a term of thirty-one years, and that he be authorised 'to enter the houses and compel persons to afford to the sweepers access to their chimneys'. They suggested that the overseer be allowed to keep the soot. King James judged the *Petition of the Poor Chimney Sweepers of the City of London* to be 'well grounded for the safety of the City and Suburbs from casualty by fire' and proposed that someone well known and respected in the city should 'oversee those allowed for the purpose'. Unfortunately for the sweeps, the Recorder, Sir Anthony Benne, thought otherwise. Such an appointment would be 'troublesome' and 'costly', and he considered the number of chimney inspectors and sweeps in the city to be sufficient.

Apart from 'calling' the name of their trade in the streets, the sweeps waited to be hired at their favourite trading place, the Eleanor Cross. Erected by Edward I in the

Following the Great Fire of London in 1666, seen here in a view from Bankside, a number of regulations, including the banning of thatched roofs, were imposed.

thirteenth century, the cross dominated the centre of Cheapside for three and a half centuries. It was pulled down in 1643 and, twenty years later, London sweeps, still mourning their loss, published *The Chimney Sweepers' Sad Complaint*. They had found no 'speedy way' to replace their cross, their trade was declining and they bemoaned the fact that they now had to find a new 'constant place of standing'. Events, however, swiftly overtook them.

In September 1666, the Great Fire of London burned for four days and nights and twenty thousand Cheapside residents became homeless. The fire destroyed more than thirteen thousand dwellings and the city had to be rebuilt. The 1667 Re-building Act ordered that houses no longer be built of wood and that businesses that used fire – such as bakeries – be restricted to certain areas. Ranging from two to four storeys high, four types of building were specified. Not counting cellars and garrets, the first and smallest had to be two storeys high and erected in by-lanes; the second, built in streets and lanes, three storeys; the third, erected in the high streets and principal streets, four storeys with balconies. The fourth and largest type, 'the mansions of principal citizens and persons of quality', should be built 'at the discretion of the builder, provided they did not exceed four storeys'. All premises had chimneys.

The chimney sweeps ultimately benefited. By the end of the century they had established themselves at their new 'guildhall', the Little (or 'Pissing') Conduit near St Paul's, where the railings around the obsolete water-fountain provided a useful propping-place for brooms and shovels while they waited for customers.

THE EIGHTEENTH CENTURY

The beginning of the eighteenth century was the age of the classical fireplace. As the middle classes became wealthier, builders and joiners took advantage of a number of pattern books. The standard textbook was John Vardy's *Designs of Inigo Jones and William Kent* (1735). As a general calculation for fireplace construction, Vardy advised that the area of the opening at the front and sides of the fire should not exceed eight times the cross-sectional area of the flue.

Chimney-pots were added to existing stacks to increase height and improve draught, and they increased in popularity from 1760 onwards. Pots known as 'tall-boys' sometimes reached a height of 7 feet (2.1 metres). Clay pots were mostly hand-made at local brickworks. They bore either the mark of the potter's wheel or the maker's individual mark, and a variety of regional types of pot and decorative styles can still be seen around Britain. Samuel Bagster, visiting his uncle John Denton at his Brick Tile and Chimney Pot Manufactory at St Pancras in the 1780s, noted that: 'the red chimney pots', found to have 'fissures, not cracks' in them, were filled with 'Suffolk cheese and brick dust', which gave them a 'good face and a sounding ring when struck'.

The population of London doubled during the reign of George III. This led to a building boom and a proliferation of chimneys. Coal was in general use as a domestic fuel – though not in the country, where transportation costs made it too expensive to use. Coal required double the air supply of wood to get it started and 'iron chimneys' – the name given to raised baskets or grates – were manufactured and placed in the hearth.

As terraced housing became more commonplace flues became smaller. Small flues not only took less space in shared chimney-stacks but also were more efficient when

Masters trading solely as chimney sweeps displayed either a circular brush or a short, sturdy brush known as a 'Turk's head' outside their premises, as shown in the top right corner of Robert Edwards's trade card of 1757.

This chimney sweep's trade sign comprised a row of brushes and a shovel.

burning coal. An average flue measured 9 inches (23 cm) by 4 inches (10 cm) or 8 inches (20 cm) square, and a few flues where stoves were installed were known to be 6 inches (15 cm) square. Only children could sweep flues.

An increase in the number of chimneys meant that chimney sweeps were much in demand. Consequently a hierarchy developed, which was reflected in the way that the sweeps advertised their trade. High masters, affluent 'governors' with established chimney-sweeping contracts, could afford illustrated trade cards. These cards were more like handbills with the reverse side used to record payments. Governors hung painted wooden signs from their premises, dressed as gentlemen, carried the 'golden rod' (an early symbol of their trade) and visited their clients by horse and carriage.

Soot was highly prized in the eighteenth century. London soot was sold in abundance, mainly to farmers in the Home Counties, as a fertiliser for cereal crops. Soot boosted the sweeps' income and gave rise to the soot trader. One such was 'JONATHAN CROW, Chimney Sweeper: Nightman and Dealer in Soot, No 37 Cross-Street Islington'. Mr Crow also advertised another service: 'Night Work Decently Perform'd at the Shortest Notice.' His men were hired to enter the homes of his clients and remove 'night soil' from their privies. This necessary job was popular among the sweeps because it fitted in with their unsociable hours.

Prices for sweeping chimneys varied according to the rentable value of the house and type of flue. In the 1780s, 150 established master sweeps lived in London. Between them they employed two hundred journeymen and approximately 550 climbing boys. High masters provided their apprentices with truckle beds, a daily meal, and a wash and change of clothes on Sundays.

Jonathan Crow's card shows a covered horse-drawn cart. Two men carry between them a barrel containing 'night soil'. The barrel is taken up the ladder and tipped into the cart, the contents to be deposited in Fleet Ditch.

The trade card of George Cordwell (1784) reads: 'Chimney sweeper to their Royal Highness's the Dukes of Gloucester and Cumberland at the Golden Broom the top of Grosvenor Mews near Berkely Square. Extinguishes Chimneys when on fire. Fixes and cleans Coppers and Smoak Jacks. Cures smoaking Chimneys in Town and Country. (No cure no pay) and by strict attention to Business himself performs what he undertakes with the utmost care and expedition.' The golden rod, symbol of the trade, is incorporated in the frame, and at the bottom is a client with the master sweep and three apprentices.

Masters employing one or two boys or single-handed sweeps with no premises roamed the streets 'calling' for trade. They were known as 'small masters'. The high masters despised 'knullers' and 'queriers' – the sweeps who had not served an apprenticeship and went about knelling (ringing a bell) or knocking on doors. Poor sweeps often swept for the soot alone. They rented one room in a lodging house, where they lived with their wife and children. Their apprentices slept in the cellar with the soot. Small, undernourished children were perfect for sweeping narrow chimney flues.

Towards the end of the century there was growing concern about the number of children employed in the trade. In 1785 the philanthropist Jonas Hanway published *A Sentimental History of Chimney Sweepers*. Hanway was acquainted with David Porter, a prominent master sweep who lived in Marylebone. Mr Porter took regulation of the trade a step further. In 1788 he petitioned Parliament on behalf of the sweeps and the first Chimney Sweeping Act was passed. The act decreed that the minimum age for children should be eight years. However, little notice was taken as the most important

clause – that master sweeps be registered – was dropped. On 12th August 1797, James Woodforde wrote in his diary:

> Holland the Chimney Sweeper swept my Study Chimney, Parlour ditto … and their Chamber Chimneys, with Kitchen and Back-Kitchen ditto – in all six. He had a new boy with him who had likely to have lost his life this morning at Weston House (home of Squire Custance) in sticking in one of their chimneys. I gave the poor boy a shilling.

THE EARLY NINETEENTH CENTURY

Several factors led to the – by no means universal – adoption of chimney-sweeping machines. Reputable master sweeps and members of the public were concerned about reports of children aged three and four years being forced up hot flues, and of small children being 'loaned' to unscrupulous sweeps. Subsequently, the first *Society for Superseding the Necessity for Climbing Boys* (SSNCB) was formed in London in 1803. Prompted by this society's initiative, the *Society of Arts, Manufacture, and Commerce*, now known as the Royal Society of Arts (RSA), decided to reinstate its competition for a chimney-sweeping machine. Results when first launched in 1796 had been disappointing. First prize and the society's gold medal were awarded to George Smart for his 'Scandiscope' machine. Assurance companies such as the Hand-in-Hand, who depended upon the sweep's efficiency, were among the first to promote the new machine by recommending master sweeps who used it.

On 28th June 1817, twelve Bristol chimney sweeps published an *Appeal to the Public*. The highly respectable masters assured their customers that they had 'no quarrel with machines', but 'all chimneys' could not be 'swept by machines'.

'Some wooden tubes, a brush, a rope,
Are all you need to employ;
Pray order, maids, the Scandiscope,
And not the climbing boy.'

George Smart's Scandiscope won first prize in a competition to design a machine
for sweeping chimneys in 1804.

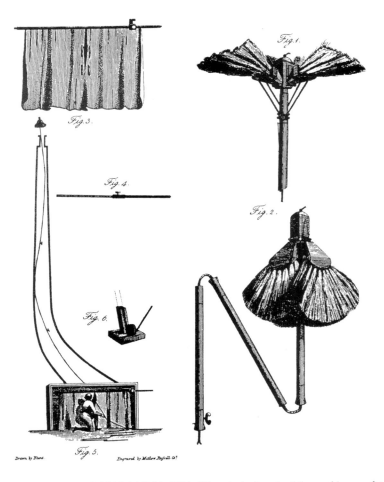

George Smart's Scandiscope, Gold Medal RSA, 1804. 'The principal parts of the machine are the brush, the rods for raising the brush, and the cord for connecting the whole together. The BRUSH consists of four fan-shaped or wing-like portions, (see fig 1 and 2) which are hung upon hinges, in order that in ascending the chimney the brush may take up as little space as possible, and in descending may spread out and sweep the sides of the flue; by contrivance exactly like what is made for umbrellas. The RODS are hollow tubes, with a metal socket at the lower end; some of the sockets have a ferew in them for the purpose of confining the cord, and preventing the rods from separating (see fig. 2). Two feet and a half is found a very convenient length for each rod. The CORD runs from the top of the brush, through all the rods, and when drawn tight, keeps the whole of the machine together.'

Smart's machine was surpassed in 1828 by the invention of Joseph Glass, a builder from Cripplegate. Glass's chimney-sweeping machine was made of solid, but pliable, cane rods with brass screw joints that when put together formed one connecting rod. Glass claimed to have superintended 'the sweeping of nearly 30,000 chimneys in the metropolis' and his machine won the approval of the SSNCB and Parliament. The machine proved to be adequate in straight flues, but horizontal flues known as 'flats', running up to 30 feet (9 metres), could be swept only by small children.

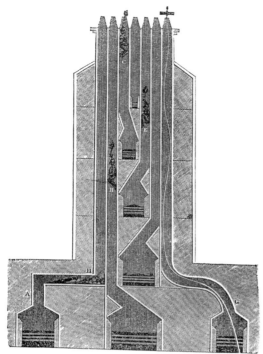

Left: *In 1828 Joseph Glass invented a 'machine' that is the prototype of the present-day equipment. He described it as follows: 'Solid cane with brass screw joints, when put together form one connecting rod with a good brush on the top of which a wheel is fixed. In the machine, the brush (at the top of flue G) is laid on the grate. The chimney cloth is then fixed on the fireplace with a slide and case, without rods or forks (usual method of propping up the cloth). The rods are then attached to the brush, through a sleeve in the centre of the cloth, and one put on in succession, till the brush reaches the top of the flue. The sweep employed is well aware when the brush passes through the chimney-pot by the springing of the machine. As the rods are detached, the machine is worked up and down. By which means the flue is thoroughly cleaned. Price, plus cloth: 80 feet in length – £5, 60 feet – £4, 40 feet - £3.' This diagram contrasts his invention in the right-hand flue with the positions of boys in the other flues.*

Right: *This monument in Church Litten Park, Newport, Isle of Wight, reads: 'To the memory of Valentine Gray, The little sweep, Interred January 5th AD 1822 In the 10th Year Of his age.' Valentine, an orphan from Alverstoke workhouse, was healthy and well when he was apprenticed by a local master sweep called Davis. Several months later Valentine was found dead in an outhouse. Davis and his wife were convicted of manslaughter and imprisoned for one year. An arcade of shops in Newport has been named Gray's Walk in memory of the little sweep.*

Of the two hundred masters and five hundred apprentice sweeps in London at the beginning of the nineteenth century, there were twenty or so high masters, averaging five apprentices each and 150 journeymen. The middle classes, who owned an estimated ninety thousand homes, had their flues swept four times a year.

Prices for sweeping chimneys ranged from 6d to 1 shilling (2.5–5p) for a large flue. Kitchen chimneys where stoves were installed contained flues that were 7 or sometimes 6 inches (17 or 15 cm) square. Chimney sweeps such as John Whitney from Leadenhall Street, who advertised 'machines or small boys, for register stoves', and others needing 'small heads for small flues' could buy a tiny child from an impoverished widow, or an orphan from a parish overseer. The usual price was £3 or £4. Children were

21

By the Chimney Sweeping Act of 1834, any person crying 'sweep' in the streets was liable to a penalty of 40 shillings.

sometimes placed with uncaring masters and there were a number of reported cases of cruelty.

When a second Chimney Sweeping Act was passed in 1834, the act raised the age of consent for climbing chimneys to ten years and restricted the number of apprentices per master to four. Once again, there were no provisions to enforce the law.

An air of mystery surrounded the sweeps. Other children regarded young sweeps of their own age with a mixture of fascination and fear. Some were envious. Children of the gentry, alarmed by the sweeps' black appearance, were terrified they might be 'given to the sweeps' if they misbehaved. Dickens, recalling his childhood, remembers 'a little sweep' about his own age, with curly hair and white teeth, whom he 'devoutly and sincerely believed to be the lost son and heir to some illustrious personage'. To his disappointment, Dickens discovered that the boy was never claimed but eventually 'settled down as a master sweep in the neighbourhood of Battle Bridge' (King's Cross).

Above and right: The 1834 act also decreed that apprentices wear a brass badge, curved to fit the forehead. This was attached to the front of a climbing cap and showed the name, address and services offered by the sweep. This apprentice badge reads 'James Taylor, Chimney Sweeper, Flue, Smoak Jack Cleaner, No. 35 King Street, Cheltenham'. It measures 7 by 4 inches (18 by 10 cm) and is part of the chimney-sweep collection at Leeds Industrial Museum.

Chimney sweeps at the Northumberland races in 1826.

In mines and factories, children worked sixteen-hour shifts and hardly saw the light of day. Chimney flues were swept before householders awoke and a young sweep's working day could begin as early as four o'clock in the morning. Afternoons, however, were free. This was because their masters were occupied visiting clients and young apprentices were not strong enough to sift soot – an afternoon job carried out by older journeymen.

Illustrators of the day show young sweeps eating and drinking on the streets, teasing passers-by, boxing, gambling, attending cockfights and the theatre, going to the races and participating in Donkey Derbies.

Many philanthropists and members of the gentry befriended the young sweeps. Captain Budsworth in Bristol and Elizabeth Montagu, Charles Lamb and Captain Southgate in London all treated the apprentice sweeps of their neighbourhood to an annual feast consisting of roast beef and plum pudding. Others took care of their spiritual welfare by providing soap and a change of clothes so that they could attend church on Sunday. Young sweeps, moreover, did well with 'perks' and annual celebrations.

THE VICTORIAN ERA

When Victoria became Queen in 1837, Societies for Superseding the Necessity for Climbing Boys had sprung up in many towns and cities, and Charles Dickens started publishing instalments of *Oliver Twist; A Parish Boy's Progress*. In the novel, Mr Gamfield takes Oliver before the magistrate to be indentured into his ''spectable chimbley-sweepin' bisness'. Queen Victoria agreed to become a patron of the London SSNCB in 1838. At that time, the secretary Robert Stevens reported that machines had swept more than 22,000 chimneys in the capital. The chimneys were in public buildings such as the Bank of England (170 flues), East India Company (220 flues) and St Thomas's Hospital (329 flues). Awkward angles in flues had been rounded off, or an opening 6 inches (15 cm) or 9 inches (23 cm) square had been built into the flue and fitted with an iron soot-door. Costing from 8 shillings (40p) to 10 shillings (50p) each, soot-doors were too expensive for the average householder.

Arguments for and against machines continued. In the cities, master sweeps with big contracts could afford machines and the higher wages of men employed to use them. Opposition was stronger in the country, where poorer masters complained that brushes were costly, they frequently broke, or they stuck in the flue and a boy had to be sent up. As recorded in a Report from Parliamentary Papers, the masters argued that 'a man with 6 children could get through more work in a day' than he could 'with a machine'. Furthermore, they feared for their trade, 'as anyone could use a machine' (Evidence before Parliament).

Above: *The flue from a corner fireplace in the officer's pantry in the Bank of England, in 1842, one of thirteen such flues fitted with a soot-door to work the brushes through. The door cost 9 shillings. Similar arrangements were made to flues in Buckingham Palace, the Post Office and Ironmongers' Hall.*

'Pity the poor climbing boys!' Arriving early in the morning before the household was up, this boy is too small to reach the knocker. He carries two kinds of scraper and a large soot sack. He would kick off his shoes before climbing the flue.

The 1840 Chimney Sweeping Act banned the climbing of chimneys by apprentices under the age of twenty-one years and imposed a fine of 'not more than £10 or less than £5' for entering the flue to extinguish a fire.

Lord Ashley (later Earl of Shaftesbury) intervened in 1840, and a third Chimney Sweeping Act was passed. The act banned the apprenticing of boys under the age of sixteen years. There were other restrictions but they were mostly ignored. Select Committees, meeting to discuss the issue, were told repeatedly that magistrates themselves and gentry generally preferred boys, and so did members of Parliament. Indeed, while they were debating the issue, young apprentice sweeps were still climbing the Westminster flues.

In the 1840s a chimney sweep named Edwards lived in John Wesley's old house in Orchard Street, London. He used the chapel at the back as a soot warehouse. There were approximately 300,000 houses in London. Each household burned approximately 4 tons of coal annually. Chimneys were swept generally four times a year, and the amount of soot collected was a million bushels (a bushel being a dry measure of 8 gallons).

'The pursuit of knowledge under difficulties.' Many apprentices taught themselves to read and write.

In 1841, the number of chimney sweeps in Britain totalled 5028. More than 120 of them were widows who had taken over their husbands' businesses. There were eight hundred adult sweeps in and around London. They employed four hundred journeymen and sixty-two boys. A large proportion of their income still came from the sale of soot.

Because so many sweeps were needed, single-handed masters could afford rented premises. With a fixed establishment they were able to take on apprentices and advertise their trade. A young sweep's life could be hazardous. Less agile children might lose their way in flues and be overcome by fumes or suffocate in soot. Other unfortunates risked life or limb when tumbling from roofs in broken pots. Adventurous children – there were many instances of girls being employed – took pride in their climbing prowess. With little opportunity for schooling, many taught themselves to read and write.

An apprentice lived with his master until he became a journeyman. He then had the option to stay or set up his own business. Boys who were 'out of their time' or who grew too big to climb were free to take other employment. Some favoured the Merchant Navy. Mostly, though, apprentice sweeps remained in the trade. Generations of sweeps, such as the Pearce family who are still operating in south-east England, can trace their chimney-sweeping ancestry back to the early seventeenth century.

Industrial expansion led to a greater reliance on coal. By mid century, one-quarter of general trade on the Thames was taken up with coal, and more domestic chimneys were built. Before lighting a fire in a new chimney, the flue had to be 'cored'. To do this, an apprentice sweep climbed through the flue removing building debris; an impossible task for a machine. Coring was also carried out in old

George Elson remembered coring new chimneys in St Bernard Abbey, Charnwood, Leicestershire, during his climbing days in the 1840s. While he climbed through each one his master would wait on the roof to help in case he got into difficulties. This illustration is by George Cruikshank.

chimneys that had been coated with a lime mortar. Wood burning caused no problems, but the gases generated by burning coal destroyed the mortar.

Stately homes and mansions posed particular problems for the machine. In 1862, Buckinghamshire master sweep Henry Swift told a Parliamentary Committee that he had been employed – against his conscience – to use a boy in a flue that ran round 'three sides of a room, probably with a view to airing it'. Another example was the kitchen part of Carlton Hall, Cambridgeshire. The local sweep who swept the chimneys with his son and other boys explained that where the tower stood there

A display of Victorian chimney-pots at Avoncroft Museum, Bromsgrove, Worcestershire.

One of Linley Sambourne's illustrations for the 1898 edition of Charles Kingsley's 'The Water Babies', first published in 1863, which drew attention to the plight of chimney sweeps' apprentices.

were twenty-three chimneys. The chimneys went up about 60 feet (18 metres), then descended about 45 feet (14 metres), then went flat, then rose again about 50 feet (15 metres).

Charles Kingsley's *The Water Babies* was published in 1863, and Kingsley's tale of young Tom's escape from chimney sweep Mr Grimes did much to arouse public sympathy. Shaftesbury intervened again and a fourth Chimney Sweeping Act was passed in 1864. Even so, the act was still ignored and it was not until the passing of the Education Act in 1870 and the licensing of sweeps in the fifth and final Chimney Sweeping Act of 1875 that machines finally superseded the climbing boys.

A Contract costs from One Guinea and upwards per annum, according to the size of the house and work involved, e.g., the usual charges for a house of about 18 or 20 rooms on 6 floors (including basement), such as Cornwall Gardens, St. George's Square, Westbourne Terrace, etc., would be as follows, viz.:—

	£	s.	d.
The Kitchen chimney swept eight times a year, at 2s. 6d. each time, equals	1	0	0
Three Basement (Pantry, Servants' Hall, and House-keeper's Room) twice a year 1s. 6d. each, equals	0	9	0
Two Dining Rooms and two Drawing Rooms twice a year at 1s. 6d. each time, equals	0	12	0
Say six other rooms once a year at 1s., equals ...	0	6	0
Or a total for the Year of ...	£2	7	0

Whereas the Company's Charge for an Annual Contract for such a house is usually about 35/- a year, or a saving of over 25 per cent.

Prices charged by the Ramoneur company for chimney-sweeping in 1914.

28

THE TWENTIETH CENTURY

Life for the sweeps remained much the same until the First World War. On country estates such as Hatfield, Hertfordshire, where there were over two hundred chimneys, local sweeps still earned a good living. Generally, though, sweeps were called less often. Coal fires continued to burn downstairs, but newly installed gas fires proved more efficient when heating bedrooms. Soot still had its uses. 'Best soot' that was obtained solely from coal fires had become scarce and artificial fertilisers gradually replaced traditional manure. Sweeps nevertheless sold an abundance of soot. In 1930, agricultural records show that 4600 tons of soot were used on Hertfordshire farmland.

By the Second World War the image of the sweep had changed dramatically. Great power stations had been built, and cheap electricity enabled householders to heat their homes with the electric bar fire. Sweeps had to travel further for customers. Enterprising sweeps took advantage of motorised transport; they wore white coats, offered clean, efficient services and used the sides of their vans to advertise their business premises.

When areas of London and other cities were devastated during the war, people were quickly rehoused in high-rise apartment blocks, and pipe-like flues replaced chimneys.

There were 471 listed chimney sweeps in London in the 1950s. Thirty years later, numbers were reduced to eighty-eight. A major disaster and two acts of Parliament brought about a decline in trade. In the great smog of 1952, four thousand Londoners died, and something had to be done about air pollution. Consequently the 1956 and 1968 Clean Air Acts were passed. In smoke-control areas such as London and Manchester no wood or coal fires were allowed. Homes had to be heated instead with authorised solid fuels, gas and electricity. Oil-burning appliances were permitted as long as they were well maintained. Local-authority grants were available, and a householder would be given six months to convert an old grate or install a new one. Furthermore, building regulations in 1965 required all chimneys to be lined.

The story of Cyril Firkins of Palmers Green in north London typifies the experience of chimney sweeps after the

MITCHELL'S CIGARETTES

DOMESTIC HEATING, 1837 & 1937

This cigarette card highlights the changes facing sweeps during the inter-war years.

Second World War. He began working for his father in 1942, 'pushing his barrow around the streets of London'. The business, which was established in 1860, employed nine men and owned six motor vehicles. After the Clean Air Acts the business was reduced to Cyril, his brother and two vans. The firm's soot trade continued, however, until the 1970s. Firkins & Sons now includes Cyril's son, Graham.

A revival in chimney-building came in the 1980s. A home, after all, is where the hearth is. Many fireplaces were unblocked and new regulations in 1985 recommended that flues be built 8 inches (20 cm) or a preferred 9 inches (23 cm) square.

To help with their extra workload, chimney sweeps in the twenty-first century use

an extra item of equipment, the vacuum cleaner. The machine is used to remove soot from the hearth, the entire length of the flue having been swept first by rods and a suitably sized brush head.

There were approximately two thousand working sweeps in Britain in 2002, and they have their own trade association. The National Association of Chimney Sweeps (NACS) was formed in 1982 to promote the sweeps' professional image. Registered members, who have passed the requisite examinations at the Chimney Training Centre at Stone, Staffordshire, work to a code of practice that ensures that they use the correct size brushes

The Numatic range of vacuum cleaners for soot removal.

Right and below: *Jim Welling, from Tring, Hertfordshire, has been a sweep for over twenty-five years. His father was a Berkhamsted carrier who took coke to London and returned with soot for the local farmers. Mr Welling uses tubular polypropylene rods and an industrial vacuum cleaner. A brush head lasts about four months and the rods about six months.*

and issue a chimney safety certificate on completion of the job. The sweeps meet annually with associated trades, and their Chimney Works Trade Show is attended by sweeps from the United States of America and Europe. Their proud tradition is upheld every year in Rochester, Kent, when sweeps from all parts of Britain take part in the Chimney Sweeps' May Day Parade.

Sweeps at their trade show in 2002 wearing their wedding-day outfits. Throughout the centuries, chimney sweeps have been associated with good fortune. Tradition has it that a sweep's presence at a wedding will bring the couple good luck. This was a popular belief in Victorian times that is still upheld.

FURTHER READING

British Parliamentary Papers, Session No. 13, 1863: *Report from the Committee of the House of Commons*.

Clavering, Robert. *Construction and Building of Chimneys*. I. Taylor, London, 1779, 1788, 1793.

Clifton-Taylor, A. *Pattern of English Building*. Faber, 1972.

Cullingford, Benita. *British Chimney Sweeps: Five Centuries of Chimney Sweeping*. The Book Guild, 2000; Ivan R. Dee, USA, 2001.

Dunning, G.C. 'Medieval Chimney Pots', from chapter 5, *Studies in Building History*, Brighton Library, 1961.

Fletcher, Valentine. *Chimney Pots and Stacks*. Centaur Press, 1994.

Hanway, Jonas. *A Sentimental History of Chimney Sweepers*. 1785.

Mayhew, Henry. *London Labour and the London Poor*. Three volumes, 1851. New impression, *Mayhew's London*, Hamlyn Publishing, 1967.

McDonald, Roxana. *The Fireplace Book*. Architectural Press, 1984.

Porter, David. *Considerations on the Present State of Chimney Sweepers*. London, 1792.

Remembracia, The City of London Records, 1579–1664, iv, 30, page 67.

Williams, Keith. *Stoves, Hearths and Chimneys*. David & Charles, 1992.

Wood, Margaret E. *The English Medieval House*. HarperCollins, 1981.

USEFUL ADDRESSES

Many historic houses have a range of elaborate chimneys and some castle rooms still have fireplaces in their walls, but the only collection of chimney-sweep material is held at the *Leeds Industrial Museum,* Armley Mills, Canal Road, Leeds LS12 2QF (telephone: 0113 263 7861; website: www.leeds.gov.uk/armleymills). This is Dr Sydney Henry's collection of books and illustrations relating to chimney sweeps, donated in 1956. To view the material, telephone 0113 263 7861 for an appointment.

National Association of Chimney Sweeps (NACS), Unit 15, Emerald Way, Stone Business Park, Stone, Staffordshire ST15 0SR. Visitors should first telephone 01785 811732. Website: www.chimneyworks.co.uk

National Fireplace Association, 6th Floor, The McLaren Building, 35 Dale End, Birmingham B4 7LN. Telephone: 0121 200 1310. Website: www.nfa.org.uk

The Solid Fuel Association, 7 Swanwick Court, Alfreton, Derbyshire DE55 7AS. Telephone: 0845 601 4406. Website: www.solidfuel.co.uk